M000215462

the farm

THE FARM

Wendell Berry

drawings by
Carolyn Whitesel

Counterpoint
Berkeley/California

Copyright (c) 1995 by Wendell Berry
Drawings copyright (c) 1995
by Carolyn Whitesel
First Counterpoint edition: 2018

ISBN: 978-1-64009-095-8

The first Counterpoint edition is a faithful
reproduction of the letterpress
limited edition designed and composed
by Gray Zeitz at Larkspur
Press in Monterey, Kentucky, in 1995.

COUNTERPOINT
2560 Ninth Street, Suite 318
Berkeley, CA 94710
www.counterpointpress.com

Printed in Canada
Distributed by Publishers Group West

1 3 5 7 9 10 8 6 4 2

Go by the narrow road
Along the creek, a burrow
Under shadowy trees
Such as a mouse makes through
Tall grass, so that you may
Forget the paved road you
Have left behind, and all
That it has led to. Or,
Best, walk up through the woods,
Around the valley rim,
And down to where the trees
Give way to cleared hillside,
So that you reach the place
Out of the trees' remembrance
Of their kind; seasonal
And timeless, they stand in
Uncounted time, and you

Have passed among them, small
As a mouse at a feast,
Unnoticed at the feet
Of all those mighty guests.
Come on a clear June morning
As the fog lifts, trees drip,
And birds make everywhere
Uninterrupted song.

*h*owever you may come,
You'll see it suddenly
Lie open to the light
Amid the woods: a farm
Little enough to see
Or call across—cornfield,
Hayfield, and pasture, clear
As if remembered, dreamed

And yearned for long ago,
Neat as a blossom now
When all its fields are mowed
And dew is fresh upon it,
Bird music all around.
That is the vision, seen
As on a Sabbath walk:
The possibility
Of human life whose terms
Are Heaven's and this earth's.

Stay years if you would know
The work and thought, the pleasure
And grief, the feat, by which
This vision lives. In fall
You plow the bottomland
For corn, the heavy ground,

So frost will work the clods.
When it's too wet to plow,
Go to the woods to fell
Trees for next winter's fuel.
Take the inferior trees
And not all from one place,
So that the woods will yield
Without diminishment.
Then trim and rick the logs;
And when you drag them out
From woods to rick, use horses
Whose hooves are kinder to
The ground than wheels. In spring
The traces of your work
Will be invisible.

Near winter's end, your flock
Will bear their lambs, and you
Must be alert, out late
And early at the barn,
To guard against the grief
You cannot help but feel
When any young thing made
For life falters at birth
And dies. Save the best hay
To feed the suckling ewes.
Shelter them in the barn
Until the grass is strong,
Then turn them out to graze
The green hillsides, good pasture
With shade and water close.
Then watch for dogs, whose sport
Will be to kill your sheep

And ruin all your work.
Or old Coyote may
Become your supper guest,
Unasked and without thanks;
He'll just excerpt a lamb
And dine before you know it.
But don't, because of that,
Make war against the world
And its wild appetites.
A guard dog or a jenny
Would be the proper answer;
Or use electric fence.
For you must learn to live
With neighbors never chosen
As with the ones you chose.
Coyote's song at midnight
Says something for the world
The world wants said. And when

You know your flock is safe
You'll like to wake and hear
That wild voice sing itself
Free in the dark, at home.

*a*s the fields dry, complete
Your plowing; you must do this
As early as you can.
Then disk and drag the furrows.
And now the past must come
To serve the future: dung
And straw from the barn floor
You carry to the fields,
Load after load until
The barns are clean, the cropland
All covered with manure.
In early May, prepare

The corn ground, plant the corn.
And now you are committed.
Wait for the seed to sprout,
The green shoots, tightly rolled,
To show above the ground
As risen from the grave.
Then you must cultivate
To keep them free of weeds
Until they have grown tall
And can defend themselves.

*W*here you grew corn last year,
Sow buckwheat, let it seed,
Then disk it in and grow
A second crop to disk in.
This is for humus, and
To keep out weeds. It is

12

A Sabbath for the land,
Rest and enrichment, good
For it, for you, for all
The ones who're yet unborn;
The land must have its Sabbath
Or take it when we starve.
The ground is mellow now,
Friable and porous: rich.
Mid-August is the time
To sow this field in clover
And grass, to cut for hay
Two years, pasture a while,
And then return to corn.

But don't neglect your garden.
Household economy
Makes family and land

13

An independent state.
Never buy at a store
What you can grow or find
At home—this is the rule
Of liberty, also
Of neighborhood. (And be
Faithful to local merchants
Too. Never buy far off
What you can buy near home.)
As early as you can,
Plant peas, onions, and greens,
Potatoes, radishes,
Cabbage and cauliflower,
Lettuce, carrots, and beets—
Things that will stand the frost.
Then as the weather warms
Plant squashes, corn, and beans,
Okra, tomatoes, herbs,

Flowers—some for yourself
And some to give away.
In the corn field plant pole beans,
Pumpkins, and winter squash;
Thus by diversity
You can enlarge the yield

*Y*ou have good grass and hay,
So keep a cow or two.
Milk made from your own grass
Is cheap and sweet. A cow
To milk's a good excuse
To bring you home from places
You do not want to be.
Fatten the annual calf
For slaughter. Keep a pig
To rescue scraps, skimmed milk,

And other surpluses.
Keep hens who will make eggs
And meat of offal, insects,
A little of your corn.
Eat these good beasts that eat
What you can't eat. Be thankful
To them and to the plants,
To your small, fertile homeland,
To topsoil, light, and rain
That make you what you are.

*B*e thankful and repay
Growth with good work and care.
Work done in gratitude,
Kindly, and well, is prayer.
You did not make yourself,
Yet you must keep yourself

By use of other lives.
No gratitude atones
For bad use or too much.

*t*his is not work for hire.
By this expenditure
You make yourself a place;
You make yourself a way
For love to reach the ground.
In its ambition and
Its greed, its violence,
The world is turned against
This possibility,
And yet the world survives
By the survival of
This kindly working love.

And while you work your fields
Do not forget the woods.
The woods stands by the field
To measure it, and teach
Its keeper. Nature is
The best farmer, for she
Preserves the land, conserves
The rain; she deepens soil,
Wastes nothing; and she is
Diverse and orderly.
She is our mother, teacher,
And final judge on earth.
The farm's a human order
Opening among the trees,
Remembering the woods.
To farm, live like a tree
That does not grow beyond

The power of its place.
A tree stands in its place
And rises by the strength
Of local soil and light,
Aspiring to no height
That it has not attained.
More time, more light, more rain
Will make it grow again
Till it has realized
All that it can become,
And then it dies into
More life, deserving more
By not desiring more.

*T*he year's first fullness comes
To the hayfields. In May,
Watching the sky, you mow

Your fields before the grass
Toughens and while the clover
Stands in its early bloom.
But weather's iffy here
In May, and in these close
Valleys, the early cutting
Is hard to cure. Some rain
Will fall on swath or windrow,
As like as not, to darken
The hay. 'It beats a snowball,'
You say then to console
Yourself, and look ahead
To later cuttings, lighter,
Better, quicker to dry.
In summer, thus, you think
Of winter, load the barns
In heat against the cold,
The January days

When you'll go out to feed,
Your breath a little cloud,
The blue air glittery
With frost. On the tracked snow
On ground that's frozen hard
You free the smell of summer
From bales of hay thrown down
Before the hungry stock.

Soon you have salad greens
Out of the garden rows,
Then peas, early potatoes,
Onions, beets, beans, sweet corn.
The bounty of the year
Now comes in like a tide:
Yellow summer squashes,
Pole beans from the cornfield,

Tomatoes, okra, eggplant,
Cabbage and cauliflower.
Eat, and give to the neighbors;
Preserve for wintertime.
Plant more, and fight the weeds.
Later will come the fall crops:
Turnips, parsnips, more greens,
The winter squashes, cushaws,
And pumpkins big as tubs.
'Too much for us,' you'll say,
And give some more away—
Or try to; nowadays,
A lot of people would
Rather work hard to buy
Their food already cooked
Than get it free by work.

Best of all is the fruit,
Sweetest and prettiest:
The strawberries and cherries,
The gooseberries and currants,
Raspberries and blackberries
(The best are wild), grapes, pears,
Apples early and late—
These gleamings in the sun
That gleam upon the tongue
And gleam put up in jars
And gleam within the mind.

Of all your harvests, those
Are pleasantest that come
Freest: blackberries from
Wild fencerows, strawberries

You happen on in crossing
The green hillsides in June;
Wild cherries and wild grapes,
Sour at first taste, then sweet;
Persimmons and blackhaws
That you gather and eat
On days you walk among
The red and yellow leaves;
And walnuts, hickory nuts
Gathered beneath the trees.
In your wild foragings
The earth feeds you the way
She feeds the beasts and birds.

*a*nd all the summer long
You're putting up more hay;
You clip the pastures, keep

The fences up, repair
Your buildings, milk your cows;
You wean the lambs; you move
The livestock to new grass;
And you must walk the fields
With hoe in hand, to cut
The thistles and the docks.
There is no end to work—
Work done in pleasure, grief,
Or weariness, with ease
Of skill and timeliness,
Or awkwardly or wrong,
Too hurried or too slow.
One job completed shows
Another to be done.
And so you make the farm
That must be daily made
And yearly made, or it

Will not exist. If you
Should go and not return
And none should follow you,
This clarity would be
As if it never was.
But praise, in knowing this,
The Genius of the place,
Whose way forgives your own,
And will resume again
In time, if left alone.
You work always in this
Dear opening between
What was and is to be.

And so you make the farm,
And so you disappear
Into your days, your days

Into the ground. Before
You start each day, the place
Is as it is, and at
The day's end, it is as
It is, a little changed
By work, but still itself,
Having included you
And everything you've done.
And it is who you are,
And you are what it is.
You will work many days
No one will ever see;
Their record is the place.
This way you come to know
That something moves in time
That time does not contain.
For by this timely work
You keep yourself alive

35

As you came into time,
And as you'll leave: God's dust,
God's breath, a little Light.

*t*o rest, go to the woods
Where what is made is made
Without your thought or work.
Sit down; begin the wait
For small trees to grow big,
Feeding on earth and light.
Their good result is song
The winds must bring, that trees
Must wait to sing, and sing
Longer than you can wait.
Soon you must go. The trees,
Your seniors, standing thus
Acknowledged in your eyes,

Stand as your praise and prayer.
Your rest is in this praise
Of what you cannot be
And what you cannot do.
But make your land recall,
In workdays of the fields,
The Sabbath of the woods.
Although your fields must bear
The barbed seed of the Fall,
Though nations yet make war
For madness and for hire,
By work in harmony
With the God-given world
You bring your days to rest,
Remain a living soul.
In time of hate and waste,
Wars and rumors of wars,
Rich armies and poor peace,

Your blessed economy,
Beloved sufficiency
Upon a dear, small place,
Sings with the morning stars.

*a*utumn ripens the corn.
You pick the yellow ears,
Carry them from the field,
Rich, satisfying loads.
The garden's final yield
Now harvested, the ground
Worked and manured, prepared
For spring, put out of mind,
You must saw, split, bring in,
And store your winter wood.
And thus the year comes round.

WENDELL BERRY, an essayist, novelist, and poet, has been honored with the T. S. Eliot Prize, the Aiken Taylor Award for poetry, the John Hay Award of the Orion Society, and the Richard C. Holbrooke Distinguished Achievement Award of the Dayton Literary Peace Prize, among others. In 2010, he was awarded the National Humanities Medal by Barack Obama, and in 2016, he was the recipient of the Ivan Sandrof Lifetime Achievement Award from the National Book Critics Circle. He is also a fellow of the Academy of Arts and Sciences. Wendell lives with his wife, Tanya Berry, on their farm in Henry County, Kentucky.